Antonín Dvořák

Chamber Works for
Piano and Strings

Antonín Dvořák

Chamber Works for Piano and Strings

Piano Trio in F Minor, Op. 65
Dumky Trio, Op. 90
Piano Quartet in D Major, Op. 23
Piano Quartet in E-flat Major, Op. 87
Piano Quintet in A Major, Op. 81

DOVER PUBLICATIONS, INC.
NEW YORK

Published in Canada by General Publishing Company, Ltd., 30 Lesmill Road, Don Mills, Toronto, Ontario.

Published in the United Kingdom by Constable and Company, Ltd., 10 Orange Street, London WC2H 7EG.

This Dover edition, first published in 1988, is a republication of portions of Series IV (Chamber Music) of *Souborné Vydání děl Antonína Dvořáka (Complete Edition of Antonín Dvořák's Works)*, originally published by Společnost Antonína Dvořáka, Státní Nakladatelství Krásné Literatury, Hudby a Umění, Prague, 1955–1958. The Czech and French versions of the editorial notes have been omitted, and a table of contents has been added.

Manufactured in the United States of America
Dover Publications, Inc., 31 East 2nd Street, Mineola, N.Y. 11501

Library of Congress Cataloging-in-Publication Data

Dvořák, Antonín, 1841–1904.
  [Chamber music. Selections]
  Chamber works for piano and strings.

  Reprint. Originally published: Souborné vydání. Prague : Artia, 1955–1959. v. 9–11. Czech and French editorial notes omitted, table of contents added.
  Contents: Piano trio in F minor, op. 65—Dumky trio, op. 90— Piano quartet in D major, op. 23—[etc.]
  1. Piano trios—Scores. 2. Piano quartets—Scores. 3. Piano quintets—Scores.
M178.D95C5   1988   88-750384
ISBN 0-486-25663-4

CONTENTS

EDITORIAL NOTES

TRIO IN F MINOR

Critical edition based on original sources and prepared for the press by the Editing Board for the Works of Antonín Dvořák: Otakar Šourek, František Bartoš, Chairman - Jan Hanuš, Chief Editor - Dr Jiří Berkovec - Jarmil Burghauser - Dr Antonín Čubr - Ladislav Láska - Antonín Pokorný - Karel Šolc.

THE THIRD PIANO TRIO, in F minor, is the 65th—originally the 64th—work of *Antonín Dvořák* (8. IX. 1841—1.V. 1904) and was completed in its first version between February 4th and March 31st, 1883, in Prague. The first movement was completed on the 19th February, the Adagio, on the 6th March, the Scherzo was begun on the 7th March and the Finale was begun on the 20th and completed on the 31st March, 1883. Just before writing it Dvořák had passed through a short but, for him, unusual pause in his creative activities. The Trio in F minor begins a new spurt of composing which produced some of Dvořák's most outstanding works marked by an atmosphere of dark, almost balladic gloom contrasted with clear-cut defiance so unlike the joyful liveliness which is otherwise so typical of Dvořák's work. During this period which reached its highwater mark with the great D minor symphony, op. 70, Dvořák passed through a period of both private and public distress such as the death of his mother (15th December, 1882), the tragic fate of his father, the great difficulties which arose in connection with the première of the opera, Dimitrij, and especially the renewed discussions concerning the foreign use of his dramatic works, all of which deeply disturbed the composer and played upon his most sensitive feelings. Dvořák fought these influences by producing a number of works all of which express the pride, independence and infallible energy and determination with which he overcame all difficulties. It was not by accident that this period of emotional tension in Dvořák's life gave us some of his most sincere and masterly compositions.

The piano trio in F minor undoubtedly holds a place among the best of Dvořák's chamber works. It is concise in expression and unusually rich in ideas which are firmly welded into a concentrated whole. The structural conception of the movements which are gloomy in spirit and which eventually win through to a more energetic and brighter mood is built up from the dark, passionate slow movement to the triumphant finale, making the work unconventional and unusual in form.

The trio did not at first assume its final form. The original version which was probably inspired directly by the above mentioned unhappy events in Dvořák's private and public life was on a larger scale and further developed, also more romantic and more varied and rich in ideas. However, before Dvořák presented the work to the public, he revised and altered it to such an extent that he produced what may be called a new work. Dvořák not only changed the order of the two middle movements but altered the whole structure of the work, made many cuts, rewrote whole passages, altered the instrumentation, and worked out the expression marks, so that finally hardly a bar remained without having been altered at least in some small detail.

It will be of interest to compare the two versions (the first version will be published separately) but apart from being of the greatest interest it will also give us a significant glimpse into Dvořák's creative workshop. The comparison will show how even a composer born, unlike many, with such spontaneous creative gifts and powers of imagination that he was often blamed as being a purely intuitive composer, could sometimes show a highly developed reflexive approach. Being dissatisfied with the first draft of the work he set about rewriting it with the utmost care and lavished his skill on it to bring it to perfection before he considered it ready to be presented to the public. The unusually high quality of the final version of the trio in F minor is a splendid example of the intensifying and enriching of a work made possible after revision.

The trio was performed for the first time in its final version by *Ferdinand Lachner, Alois Neruda and the composer* at a concert given in honour of Dvořák on the 27th October, 1883 at Mladá Boleslav. The same trio performed the work soon afterwards—on the 13th November of the same year—at a concert given by the Umělecká Beseda in Prague. The Berlin publishing house of N. Simrock brought out the work at that time and also, as was usual, published a piano duet version arranged by one of the firm's proof-readers, Robert Keller.

František Bartoš

(compiled from notes by the late Otakar Šourek)

Translated by G. Thomsen

EDITORS' NOTES

SOURCES:

a) Dvořák's manuscript in the possession of his descendants. It is an oblong manuscript book 247:330 mm in size containing 58 pages of 20 stave manuscript paper enclosed in a thin light brown cover.

The title of the work is on the cover:
"*III. Trio (F moll) Op. 64*" [the opus number has been altered in pencil to 65], underneath the title is written in Czech:
/ "*for piano, violin, 'cello / composed by / Antonín Dvořák*"

With the exception of page 38 which is blank, all the pages have been used and the last four bars of the work are written on the brown cover. Pages 2—37 are numbered in ink, pencil and red pencil. The blank page is unnumbered, the rest are numbered 38—57.

At the top of the first page of the music is written:

"Trio (Op: 64. In Prague 18$\frac{4}{2}$ 83 | Antonín Dvořák"

At the end of the first movement, on page 20 is the date: *18 $\frac{19}{2}$ 83*. On pages 21—30 is the Adagio with its date of completion, *18$\frac{6}{3}$ 83*. The third movement, the scherzo (pages 31—37) gives only the date when it was begun: *$\frac{7}{3}$ 83*. At the beginning of the finale (page 38) is the date *18$\frac{20}{3}$ 83*. After the last four bars which are written on the cover is the final date: *"Fine 18$\frac{31}{3}$ 83"*.

The manuscript, which is full of alterations and additions in ink, pencil and red and blue pencil, was not used for the print.

b) The original edition by the Berlin firm of N. Simrock which is undated (published in the autumn of 1883), Edition number 8348.

As has been said in in the foreword, the manuscript differs so widely from the Simrock print that the print seems certainly to have been made either from another manuscript of Dvořák's or else from a copy in which the composer made a great deal of alterations (especially in the first and slow movements). The printer's copy could not be made available to the Editing board for the present edition. The basis of this edition is the *Simrock print* published during the com-

poser's lifetime and certainly under his personal supervision, it being also the final version of the work.

As the manuscript (a) and the Simrock edition differ so widely, all attempt at comparison has been abandoned and the original version will be published separately. Only in those places where the manuscript has been used as a source of this edition for the purpose of making clear what are obviously omissions and mistakes in the Simrock edition, have these alterations been given either in square brackets or, in the case of a more important deviation, in the Editors' Notes (Annotazioni). The most important corrections in bars 293 and 295 of the first movement were made according to the manuscript in agreement with a printed copy formerly in the possession of *Josef v. Portheim* where it is stated that Antonín Benewitz, Josef v. Portheim and the composer used the copy for a performance (probably private) which they gave on the 10th November, 1883 — in fact, before the work was first performed in Prague. In the above mentioned bars the printed version of the chords has been altered in pencil to coincide with the original manuscript and thus it also appears in this edition.

ABBREVIATIONS:

A = the manuscript
S = the Simrock edition
SN = this edition published by the State Publishing House KLHU
P = piano, m. d. — right hand, m. s. — left hand

Big numbers indicate the bar, if small numbers are added, they indicate the note of the bar; rests are not counted.

ANNOTAZIONI

I.

10, 12, Viol. Vlc.: S = senza arpegg.; SN = A
100$_8$ P, m. d., S: g^1 — [!] — c^2 — es^2; SN = A
175$_1$ P, m. s. S: H [!] — f — g — des^1; SN = A
179$_4$ Viol., S: g — des [!] — h^1 — g^2; SN = A
199$_{12}$ P, m. s. S: des — as [!]; SN = A

293 P, m. s. S: SN = A

295 P, m. s. S: SN = A

II.

86 Viol., S: —; A: p

III.

167—168 S: — A: ▭
297   S: *a tempo;* SN = A
331   P, S: *cresc.;* SN = A (vide 332!)
333   P, S: *f;* SN = A (vide 335!)
337, 338 S: senza ▭ ; SN = A

František Bartoš

DUMKAS

Critical edition based on original sources and prepared for the press by the Editing Board for the Works of Antonín Dvořák: Otakar Šourek, Chairman - Jan Hanuš, Chief Editor - František Bartoš - Dr Jiří Berkovec - Dr Antonín Čubr - Ladislav Láska - Antonín Pokorný - Karel Šolc.

"DUMKA" was the name given to Ukrainian folk-songs of a narrative character (so-called "family ballads"), of elegiac, retrospective character, and sung to the accompaniment of folk-instruments such as the "bandura", "kobza", etc. In the piano and chamber music of *Antonín Dvořák* (8. IX. 1841—1. V. 1904), there are a number of movements with this title. It seems probable, however, that the composer, in using the word "Dumka" (pl. "Dumky"), associated it in his mind with the verb "dumati", meaning "to meditate" or "recollect", rather than with the specific type of folk-art which it designates. A circumstance that speaks for this assumption is the special character of the compositions to which Dvořák gave this title and which, unlike the Ukrainian "dumka", alternate moods of retrospection and yearning with the expression of vigorous and youthful gaiety such as corresponded to the composer's mercurial and emotional temperament. In this sense it is possible to include under the title "Dumka" not only those of Dvořák's compositions actually bearing this title but also several of the undesignated "Slavonic Dances" (No. 2 of the first series and Nos. 2 and 4 of the second).

Dvořák first used the title "Dumka" in a composition for piano, op. 35, written in 1876, and then successively in the slow movement of the String Sextet, op. 48, the String Quartet in E flat major, op. 51 (1878—79), the piano "Dumka", op. 12 (1884), the slow movement of the Piano Quintet in A major, op. 81 and then, finally, in the general title of a work comprising six compositions of the character indicated above: the *"Dumkas", Trio for violin, violoncello and piano, op. 90.*

This group of "Dumkas" is not in the usual cyclic sonata form but, as in the "Slavonic Dances", a series of six miniature movements of which each is an art-stylisation of the "Dumka", in Dvořák's conception, possessing all the originality and individuality which mark the artist's sharply differentiated melodic, rhythmic and harmonic invention and the great variety and strongly characteristic colouring of his moods. Unlike the "Slavonic Dances", however, this group of "Dumkas" has a certain structural unity, while the content of the individual compositions conforms to a general plan. This is suggested by the indication *"attacca subito"* after the first two parts (contrary to a *"short interval"* after each of the three following parts), as also by the arrangement, in respect of both structure and mood, of the parts into four groups.

Dvořák began to write the "Dumkas" piano trio some time in November 1890. The autograph score (see Editors' Notes) was completed on February 12th, 1891. The whole work was composed in the composer's Prague flat in Žitná ulice, čp. 564/II.

The first performance of this work took place on April 11th 1891 at an evening held by the Měšťanská beseda (a municipal cultural society) in Prague, in celebration of the conferring of an honorary degree on the composer by the Charles University. Dvořák himself played the piano part, Professor Ferdinand Lachner and Professor Hanuš Wihan, both of the Conservatoire, taking the violin and 'cello part respectively. (This ensemble then performed the "Dumkas" at concerts given in forty-one towns in Bohemia and Moravia on a farewell tour, undertaken at the beginning of 1892, previous to the composer's departure for America.) The "Dumkas" were published in 1894 by Simrock, Berlin.

Translated by R. Samsour   Otakar Šourek

EDITORS' NOTES

SOURCES:

a) The composer's manuscript in the possession of Dvořák's heirs.

The manuscript is enclosed in black, half-linen boards and comprises 60 pages of 12-stave music paper of oblong format, 250:325 mm. In the middle of the first page is the inscription (in Czech):

"Dumky" (opus 90.)
for piano, violin and 'cello
composed by
Antonín Dvořák.

On the same page as the inscription, there are 9 bars in the key of G major, of which the first six bars are identical with second secondary theme of the "Carnival" overture (Violino I, bars 140–145) written after the "Dumkas". They are undoubtedly one of the first thematic notes for this overture.

The actual musical transcription of the "Dumkas" begins on the following page, from which the numbering runs on to page 59. The instruments are also indicated on this page: *"Violino"*, *"Cello"* and *"Piano-Forte"*. No metronomic indications are given. The manuscript contains five different dates: 30. 11. 1890 at the end of the first part, 21. 1. 1891 after the fourth part, 23. 1. 1891 at the beginning, and 31. 1. 1891 at the end, of the fifth part, and after the last bars on p. 59, there (in Czech) the note is:

Finished in Prague, 12. 2. 1891.   *Antonín Dvořák.*

The manuscript does not appear to have been used as a master copy for the first edition, which was published during Dvořák's sojourn in America.

b) The printed edition of the music publishing house, N. Simrock, G. m. b. H., Berlin (Copyright 1894 by N. Simrock, Berlin).–In this edition a number of dynamic indications are included which had been previously entered by the composer in pencil in the manuscript. In addition, Simrock's edition has many more divergences, especially in respect of phrasing and dynamic indications, but it is not known by whom they were carried out. (At this time, printer's proofs of Dvořák's compositions were evidently corrected, at Simrock's request, by Johannes Brahms.) These were tacitly authorised by the composer even though they were not contained in the manuscript.

The present edition is based on Simrock's printed edition after careful collation with the autograph. The more important deviations between the sources are listed in the "Annotazioni". Obvious misprints have been corrected and omissions put in where the Simrock edition diverges from the autograph. In addition, indications for the executant have been inserted, where missing, according to analogous passages in the autograph and printed edition. More important additions by the editors are put in square brackets [].

ABBREVIATIONS:

A   = autograph score
S   = Simrock's edition (score)
SN   = the present edition of the State Publishing House KLHU
[!] = slip in the manuscript or misprint.
Po   = Piano
m. d. = mano destra
m. s. = mano sinistra
Viol. = Violino
Vclo = Violoncello
θ = bars missing in the manuscript.
Versio I = original version, the change having been carried out by the composer in the autograph.
Large Arabic numerals indicate the bar; the small numbers beside them indicate the note (or chord) in the bar; rests are not counted.

ANNOTAZIONI

[I]

48_3 Po m. d. A: h^1; SN = S (vide 108 A, S)
$51_{1, 2}$ Po m. d. A: e^1–gis^1–h^1–d^2–e^2; SN = S
60_2 Po m. s. A: *Dis–dis*; m. d.: *fis^1–a^1–h^1–fis^2*; SN = S

82–87, 89–90 Po A: senza Ped.
89 A: –; S: *ff*
103 A: versio I: *Vivace*
105_3 Po m. s. A: *fis*; SN = S (vide 37 A, S)
128_2 Po A: vide 60_2

[II]

1 A: $^2/_4$ senza MM; S: $^4/_8$, ♩ = 46

7_1 Vclo A: –; S : *fz*

46_1 Po m. d. A: *gis¹*; SN = S (vide 42)

84 Vclo A: *arco*; SN = S

103 A: –; S: *poco rit.*

117 Viol. A: –; S: *con sordino*

121_1 Po m. d., m. s. A: –; S: ⌁

148_2 Po m. d., m. s. A: ⌁ ; S *: ten.*

158 Viol. A: –; S: *senza sord.* (vide 117)

175 Viol. A: [musical notation] ; SN = S

192–195 Po m. d. A: *senza ottava alta*

[III]

1 A: –; S: *Andante* ♩ = 69

1–2 Po m. d. A: [musical notation] ; SN = S

(98)

17 A: –; S: *Un poco più mosso*

25 A: –; S: *Meno*

32_1 Po m. d., Viol. A: –; S: ⌢

33 A: *in tempo*; S: *poco più mosso*

143, 145 Viol., Vclo A: –; S: *con sordino*

165 A: *L'istesso tempo*; S: *Allegretto*

169 A: –; S: *ritard.*

176 A: –; S: *Meno mosso*

[IV]

1–2 A: ⊖; SN = S

3 Viol A: –; S: *senza sordino, arco*

5 Vclo A: –; S: *senza sordino*

27 A: –; S: *in tempo*

46–47 A: *d moll;* S: *D dur;* SN = A (vide 147–148)

74_2 Viol A: *g¹*; SN = S

76_1 Po m. d. A: *a¹–d²–a²*; SN = S

95,99 Po m. d., m. s. A:  ; SN = S

123 A: *Tempo I.;* SN = S

125 Viol A: vide 95; SN = S

129 A: *Andante;* SN = S

143_1 Po m. s. A: *B–b;* SN = S (vide 42)

[V]

1 A: senza MM

9 Vclo A: [musical notation] ; SN = S

91 Po m. s. A: [musical notation] ; SN = S

92 Vclo A: –; S: *quasi Recit.*

98 A: segue Vi-de:

99 A, S: *in tempo;* SN: *Tempo I.*

156 A: –; S: *Più mosso, Allegro*

[VI]

9 A: –; S: *Poco più mosso*

13–15 Viol A: [musical notation] SN = S

16 A: senza ⌢

17 A: –; S: *Più mosso*

87 A: $^2/_4$ *Lento* ♩ = ♪ = [I] (Versio I A: $^2/_4$ *Andante*); SN = S

119 A: –; S: *Un poco più mosso*

126 A: Viol, Vclo: *tempo rubato;* Po: *in tempo*

174 A: –; S: *accel.*

176 A: –; S: *Vivace*

195 A: –; S: *accel.*

203 A versio I: *Presto*

Dr Antonín Čubr

PIANO QUARTET IN D MAJOR

Critical edition based on original sources and prepared for the press by the Editing Board for the Works of Antonín Dvořák: Otakar Šourek, František Bartoš, Chairman - Jan Hanuš, Chief Editor - Dr Jiří Berkovec - Jarmil Burghauser - Dr Antonín Čubr - Ladislav Láska - Antonín Pokorný - Karel Šolc.

At the turn of the year 1874–1875, *Antonín Dvořák* (September 8, 1841 — May 1, 1904), after preceding years of ferment and seeking, attained real artistic maturity and composed a work which can be counted among the most outstanding expressions of his genius. In the field of chamber music belongs here first his String Quartet in G major (with bass, originally Opus 18), which appeared at the beginning of 1875, and his Piano Trio in B flat major, Opus 21, completed May 14 of that year. Only ten days after the completion of his trio, Dvořák began work on the score of his *Piano Quartet in D major* (May 24), completing it 18 days later, on June 10, 1875. The manuscript, however, shows traces of a later revision, the exact date of which cannot be ascertained, carried out probably for the press, as it is indicated in the Editors' Notes.

While this work lacks the stirring sparkle and thoughtful verve of the two above-named compositions, its intimacy, freshness and nobility together are also a proof of what Dvořák is capable of even when there is no question of a conflict between form and content, when the uncontroversial expressive and technical sides of his art prevail. It shows that Dvořák even under these conditions is ceaselessly seeking new, personal forms for his musical expression. In his Piano Quartet in D major, we turn our attention then in this respect not only to the special arrangement of the three movement form, unusual for Dvořák, in which the scherzo and finale are joined in one movement, the features of both flowing into each other. We note in particular the comparative freedom in the development of the musical current within the individual movements which does not go as far as aimlessness or over-development which we find in many chamber music compositions of the preceding period.

The composition was first performed at a concert of the music department of the Umělecká Beseda in Prague on December 16, 1880, in Konvikt Hall. It was performed by Václav Kopta (violin), Petr Mareš (viola), Alois Neruda (violoncello) and Karel ze Slavkovských (piano). In the same year, the Piano Quartet with instrument parts was published by Schlesinger in Berlin. How this edition compares with the original manuscript, which is the property of the music department of the University Library in Prague, has been described in the Editors' Notes and Annotazioni at the end of the score of the new edition which has now been published by the State Publishing House KLHU.

Jarmil Burghauser
(from the data of the late Otakar Šourek)

Translated by Jean Němcová

EDITORS' NOTES

SOURCES:

a) The original manuscript is the property of the University Library in Prague where it is filed under the heading 59 R 113. It consists of 42 pages of 20-stave score paper measuring 310—250 mm and unnumbered scraps of score paper. The manuscript is bound, the cover semi-flexible and grey-green in color. It is enclosed within cardboard covers. On the first, unnumbered page of the manuscript there is the following inscription (in Czech) in the elaborate penmanship which, at the time of this composition, was Dvořák's habit:

Quarteto (Opus 23)
for
Piano, Violin, Viola and 'Cello
Composed by
Antonín Dvořák

The composition itself, as noted in Dvořák's own hand, begins on the next, first numbered page with the repeated inscription: *Quarteto* [sic!] In the upper right hand corner there is the date on which the composition was begun: *18 24/5 75*. The first movement finishes on page 16, and the date of its completion is *18 30/5 75*. The original, three bar version at the conclusion of the first movement is crossed out with the composer's note: *Schluß folgt auf der 41. Seite*. On this page and the succeeding scraps of score paper, the definitive conclusion of the first movement is written with the master's notation: *Schluß des ersten Satzes* and a note at the beginning of the opening bar: *Anhang*. There are absolutely no notations in the second and beginning of the third movements until the end of the composition, in which the composer notes (in Czech): *Finished June 10, 1875, Antonín Dvořák*.

None of the three movements of this composition are numbered or in any way titled; only the third movement bears the inscription: *Finale*. Also the orientation letters beginning with the letter C, are missing in the manuscript. In the second movement, between the III and IV variation, there is Dvořák's notation: *attacca*; between the IV and V variation, *attacca Variaz. 5*. Also in the third movement after the 195th bar, there is another inscription, *attacca*. All these composer's notations, despite their superfluousness, have been included both in the Schlesinger and our own edition of this composition.

In the third variation of the second movement, the composer has written (in Czech and in German): *Softly the first time, strong the second time, Das erste mal schwach, das zweit mal stark*. This inscription is scratched out with ink. After bar 126 in the third movement, there is an insert pasted into the manuscript. This insert consists of ten new bars, of which, from the original version, one bar remained in the second

half of the page, which was crossed out by the composer.

Various clefs, which the composer used in his manuscript, sometimes even erroneous, were altered in the Schlesinger edition and in some cases corrected. These alterations and corrections are adhered to in our edition as well.

It cannot be said of this manuscript that it was used as the draft for engraving.

b) The original edition by Schlesinger in Berlin, edition number 7373, copyright 1880.

The Schlesinger edition was taken as the basis of our edition, as it was published during the composer's lifetime and doubtlessly with his participation. It has been painstakingly compared with the original manuscript. More fundamental deviations between the sources are given in the Editors' Remarks (Annotazioni).

Our edition has been corrected according to the original manuscript for its obvious typographical errors and the supplementary details from the Schlesinger edition have been omitted. In addition, analogous places in both sources have been supplemented with missing minor performance marks. More important supplementary notations by the editors are given within square brackets [ ].

NOTES:

A = original manuscript
Schl. = Schlesinger edition
SN = present edition published by the State Publishing House KLHU
Po m. d., m. s. = Piano right hand, left hand
Viol. = Violin
Vla = Viola
Vlc = 'Cello
[!] = Rewritten in the original manuscript or a misprint
Vers. I. = Original version, altered by the composer in manuscript
[?] = Unclear place in original manuscript
Large Arabic numerals indicate the bars.
Rests are not counted.

ANNOTAZIONI

I

1 Po, m. d., A: ; SN = Schl.

34, 36 Vla ⎫
35   Viol. ⎬ A: ; SN = Schl.

61 Po, m. s., A: $H_1 — G$; SN = Schl.

108_7 Po, m. d., A: a-e_1 ⎫
       Po, m. s., A: A-e ⎬ ; SN = Schl.

117—118 Vlc., A: senza legato; SN = Schl.

122 Viol., A: SN = Schl.

138 Vla, A: —; Schl.: arco; SN = Schl.

147_2 Viol., A: *ff*; SN = Schl.
160_1 Vlc., A: Vers. I.: *fis*
161 Vlc., A: Vers. I.: fis_1

174 Po, m. d., Vers. I.:

192_1 Po, m. d., A: g_1-h_1-d_2-g_2; SN = Schl.

204_1 Po, m. d., A:

214_5 Po, m. s.: Schl.: *des* [!]; SN = A
216_3 Po, m. d., A: ges_1; Schl.: as_1; SN = A
217_1 Po, m. d., Schl.: g-b-es_1 [!]; SN = A

220 Viol., Vers. I.: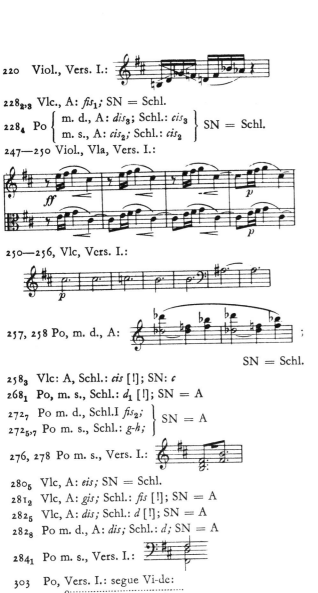

228$_{2,3}$ Vlc, A: *fis*$_1$; SN = Schl.

228$_4$ Po { m. d., A: *dis*$_3$; Schl.: *cis*$_3$; m. s., A: *cis*$_2$; Schl.: *cis*$_2$ } SN = Schl.

247—250 Viol., Vla, Vers. I.:

250—256, Vlc, Vers. I.: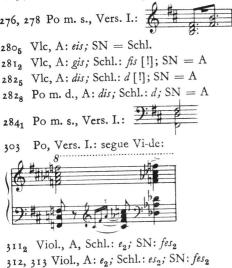

257, 258 Po, m. d., A:

SN = Schl.

258$_3$ Vlc: A, Schl.: *cis* [!]; SN: *c*

268$_1$ Po, m. s., Schl.: *d*$_1$ [!]; SN = A

272$_7$ Po m. d., Schl.I *fis*$_2$;
272$_{5,7}$ Po m. s., Schl.: *g-h*; } SN = A

276, 278 Po m. s., Vers. I.:

280$_5$ Vlc, A: *eis*; SN = Schl.

281$_2$ Vlc, A: *gis*; Schl.: *fis* [!]; SN = A

282$_5$ Vlc, A: *dis*; Schl.: *d* [!]; SN = A

282$_8$ Po m. d., A: *dis*; Schl.: *d*; SN = A

284$_1$ Po m. s., Vers. I.:

303 Po, Vers. I.: segue Vi-de:

311$_2$ Viol., A, Schl.: *e*$_2$; SN: *fes*$_2$

312, 313 Viol., A: *e*$_2$; Schl.: *es*$_2$; SN: *fes*$_2$

316—319 Po m. s., Vers. I.:

331$_3$ Po m. s., A: *a-cis*$_1$ [!]; SN = Schl.

410—412 Tutti, Vers. I.:

Allegro

II

172$_2$ Po m. s. A: *G*$_1$-*G*; SN = Schl.

17 Vers. I.: segue Vi-de: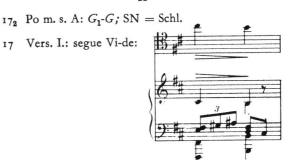

67 Vers. I.: *Meno mosso quasi tempo I.*

113$_2$ Vla, Vers. I.: *fis-d*$_1$; SN = Schl.

146 Po m. d., Vers. I.:

188 Po, A: *cresc.;* Schl.: *dim.;* SN = Schl.

197—200 Vlc, A:

III

31
226 } Tutti, A: *ff*; Schl.: *f*; SN = Schl.

59 Vers. I. segue Vi-de:

72$_1$ Po m. d., Schl.: *e-cis*$_1$; SN = A

104$_{4-6}$, 105$_{1-4}$ Po m. d., A: *stacc.;* Schl.: *legato*; SN = Schl.

115 Vers. I.: segue Vi-de:

134$_1$ Viol., Vers. I.: *e*$_3$; SN = Schl.

135$_{3-4}$ Vlc, A: *G-g*; Schl.: *Gis-gis*
135$_3$ Po m. s., A: *G-e-g*; Schl.: *Gis-e-gis* } SN = Schl.

138_2 Vla, A: *e-h-gis$_1$*; Schl.: *d-h-gis$_1$*; SN = Schl.

156_4 Viol., A: *g$_1$*; Schl. *gis$_1$*; SN = Schl.

157_1, 158_1 Vla, A:*g*; Schl.: *gis*; SN = Schl.

180_4 Viol., A: *g$_1$*; Schl.: *gis$_1$*; SN = Schl.

189 Po m. s., m. d., Schl.: *H-dis-fis-h-dis$_1$*; SN = A

306—310 Po m. d., Vers. I.:

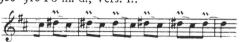

355 Po m. s., A: [?]

392_5, 394_5 Viol., Vers. I.: *e$_2$*; SN = Schl.

$394_{1,2,3}$ Vlc, Vers. I.: *d$_2$*, *fis$_2$*, *a$_1$*; SN = Schl.

407 Tutti, Vers. I.: *f*

418—419 Vlc: senza ligatura; SN = Schl.

Antonín Pokorný, Karel Šolc

PIANO QUARTET IN E FLAT MAJOR
op. 87

Critical edition based on original sources and prepared for the press by the Editing Board for the Works of Antonín Dvořák: Otakar Šourek, Chairman — Jan Hanuš, Chief Editor — František Bartoš — Dr Jiří Berkovec — Dr Antonín Čubr — Ladislav Láska — Antonín Pokorný — Karel Šolc.

THE QUARTET IN E FLAT MAJOR for violin, viola, violoncello and piano op. 87 is, after the quartet in D major op. 23 from the year 1875, *Antonín Dvořák's* (8. IX. 1841—1. V. 1904) second composition for this group of instruments. Dvořák wrote it in the year 1889 at an urgently repeated request of the Berlin publisher Fritz Simrock who first asked for a work of this kind as early as 1885 and then again at the beginning of the year 1887 (*"If you only started working on a piano quartet as you have been promising me for such a long time!"*) and in summer 1888 (*"I should like to have from you a piano quartet — and you promised it to me a long time ago! What's the matter with it?"*). Dvořák left, for a time, these suggestions unnoticed and only at the end of the year 1888, having in the meantime created a number of other compositions among which were such large scale works as the oratorio "St. Ludmilla", the second series of "Slavonic Dances", the opera "Jacobin" and others, did he promise Simrock, cautiously, that he would soon like to begin work on a piano quartet. Half a year more, however, passed before the realization of this plan. On July 10th, 1889, he began a sketch for the piano quartet in E flat major, which he completed on August 12th and at the same time from July 12th to August 19th he worked out the score.

The Piano Quartet in E flat major is, as is also the closely preceding Piano Quintet in A major op. 81 and the closely following VIIIth Symphony in G major op. 88, a work typical for that period of Dvořák's ripeness, both human and artistic, in which, after a period showing classicist tendencies, a renewed contact with the elements of Czech folk music makes itself strongly felt. At the same time it is a work typical for the period of a bright inner feeling and happily stirred mood, which at that time also gave birth to the opera "Jacobin". An artist of an expressly individual invention, who does not hesitate to deviate substantially from the accepted conventions of construction, speaks here with his music with the same convincingness as an artist full of rich inner feeling which he can show with grave decision and sincerety, but at the same time with rare nobleness and tenderness of expression.

The Quartet was performed for the first time at the 17th Popular Concert of the Umělecká Beseda, which took place in the Prague Rudolfinum on November 23rd, 1890. The performers were Hanuš Trneček (piano), Ferdinand Lachner, Petr Mareš and Hanuš Wihan (strings). The score of the quartet was published at the beginning of the same year by Simrock.

The relation of the present edition of the State Publishing House KLHU to the first edition is discussed in detail in the Editors' Notes following the last page of the music.

Translated by Dr L. Dorůžka   Otakar Šourek

EDITORS' NOTES

SOURCES:

1. The manuscript, kept in the Music Department of the National Museum in Prague, signed 857/52, comprises 54 pages of 20 stave music paper 258:330 mm in size. On the front page (which is unnumbered) there is the following inscription (in Czech):

Quartet (E flat major) for violin, viola, cello and pianoforte, composed by Antonín Dvořák, op. 87.

The first movement, beginning on the first page of the manuscript, repeats the title (in German):

Quartett, Anton Dvořák, op. 87.

The first movement ends on page 17, the second movement begins on page 18 and ends on page 27. On the same page, the third movement begins, and ends on page 38, after which the fourth movement continues up to the end. The manuscript was corrected, in red ink, by Dvořák, who also signed most of the corrections with his signature. The manuscript is bound in half-leather covers, each sheet being enclosed in a cellophane envelope.

2. The original edition by N. Simrock, Berlin, Ed. No. 9284, Copyright 1890.

Our edition is based on the Simrock print, published during the composer's lifetime and doubtlessly under his direct supervision. It has been carefully collated with the manuscript. The more important deviations between the sources are listed in the Editorial Notes ("Annotazioni"). In our edition, obvious misprints have been corrected and details omitted in the Simrock edition added in accordance with the manuscript. Further, the missing dynamic marks of minor importance and other marks pertaining to the interpretation have been added on the basis of both the manuscript and the print. The more important editors' addenda have been put within square brackets [].

ABBREVIATIONS:

A	= the manuscript
S	= Simrock's edition
SN	= the present edition of the State Publishing House KLHU
Viol.	= violin
Vla	= viola
Vclo	= violoncello
Po	= piano
[!]	= slip in the manuscript or misprint
Versio I	= original version, changed by the composer in the manuscript

Large Arabic numerals indicate the bar, the small numbers beside them indicate the note or chord in the bar. Rests are not counted.

ANNOTAZIONI

I.

1 Versio I: *Allegro risoluto;* SN = *(Allegro con fuoco)*
116 Po, A: −; S = SN: $f\!z$
235₅₋₈ Vclo, A: chiave di tenore; S = chiave di violino [!];
236₁ SN = A.

II.

66₁₆ Viol. A: *eis³;* SN = S *(gis² − eis³)*
76 Vclo A: senza arco [!]; SN = S

III.

73₃ Po, md A : $d^1-f^1-b^1$; S: $b-d^1-b^1$, SN = A
86 A: tutti strum. senza mf
195₈₋₁₀ Po, md, A: *8−va*

IV.

3₅ Vla, A: *ges¹;* SN = S *(ges¹−b¹)*
43₅ Po, md, A: ∿ ; SN = S
74 Vclo, A: ; SN = S
196₂ Viol. A: *des²* [!]; SN = S *(d²)*
218₁ Vla, A : *g¹;* SN = S *(b−g¹)*

Antonín Pokorný, Karel Šolc

QUINTET in A major

Critical edition based on original sources and prepared for the press by the Editing Board for the Works of Antonín Dvořák: Otakar Šourek, Chairman - Jan Hanuš, Chief Editor - František Bartoš - Dr Jiří Berkovec - Dr Antonín Čubr - Ladislav Láska - Antonín Pokorný - Karel Šolc.

THE QUINTET IN A MAJOR for piano, two violins, viola and violoncello, published as op. 81, was the second composition to be written by *Antonín Dvořák* (8. IX. 1841—1. V. 1904) in the same key and for the same combination of instruments. Dvořák wrote the first piano quintet in A major in the summer of 1872, in which year it was also given its first performance (22. XI. 1872). Fifteen years later, when a vain search was made for the as yet unpublished work, he decided to create a new quintet in the same key. This he did in the summer of 1887, soon after the completion of the Mass in D major, op. 76. How spontaneous was the birth of this new quintet — originally bearing the opus number 77 — may be judged from the fact that, on the 16th August, 1887, Dvořák was still able to write to his friend, Alois Göbl, at Sychrov: *"...now I am doing nothing new..."* and only two days later the date of August 18th appears on the score of the new work, the first movement of which he finished on August 28th, the whole being completed by October 3rd *"at Vysoká, on the village feast-day"*, as is noted beneath the last line of the score. (The manuscript, which is in the possession of the composer's heirs, bears no other dates.)

The rare freshness of its spontaneous creation is, however, apparent also in the work itself, which may be described as one of the most authentic and self-revealing musical portraits we possess. In it is contained the quintessence of Dvořák's personality: a man seemingly very reserved, living his life of ideas far removed from everyday things, still wandering in the Elysian fields of musical imagination, now frowningly lost in thought, now smiling and happy, full of the joy and exultation of living and creating. Here is a spirit whose moods are as numberless and changeable as the sky in spring and, above all, a genius consecrated to his art, whose soul, in closest communion with Nature, creates works of rare purity and individual beauty.

The Piano Quintet, op. 81, which has long been one of the most played chamber music compositions in world literature, was first performed at a popular concert of Dvořák's works held by the "Umělecká Beseda" on January 8th, 1888 in the Prague Rudolphinum (the present-day House of Artists). The pianist was Karel Kovařovic, and the string players, Karel Ondříček, Jan Pelikán, Petr Mareš and Alois Neruda, all members of the National Theatre orchestra. The work was published in the same year by Simrock, Berlin, with a dedication to Dr Neureuther, Professor of Medicine in the Charles University, a generous patron of the young Czech musical generation.

For this new edition, published by the State Publishing House KLHU, the score and parts of the Quintet have been carefully revised on the basis of a comparison of the first Simrock edition with the composer's manuscript; details of this revision are given in the Editor's Notes on the last page of the score.

Otakar Šourek

Translated by R. Samsour

EDITORS' NOTES

SOURCES:

a) The manuscript in the possession of Dvořák's heirs, who have kindly enabled the Committee to use it for the revision of this edition. It is enclosed in red-brown paper covers with dark crimson back and corner pieces (linen). It consists of 112 pages of music paper 308 : 238 mm in size, each sheet containing 18 staves. The title of the work (in Czech) is inscribed on the first page of the music manuscript as follows:

Vysoká 18. 8. 1887
(published by Simrock in
Berlin as opus 81.)

Quintet for piano   *(opus 77.)*
two violins, viola and cello
composed by
Ant. Dvořák

The music manuscript comprises 111 pages, the twelfth sheet in glued over; page 23 is replaced with a new version and on page 24 the original version is crossed out. New version from page 23 continues then on page 25, and from this page on, the manuscript contains twofold numbering, which either includes the deleted page, or leaves it out.

The first movement begins in the manuscript on page 1 and ends on page 38/39, under the last bar of this movement the date 28. 8. 87 is indicated. At the top of the following page the second movement entitled *(Dumka)* begins; this inscription stands in the place of the original title, which was probably different and was erased. In this movement bars 87–100 are glued over, so that it is not possible to ascertain whether the original version was changed or merely replaced with a more legible manuscript. This movement ends on page 63/64 in the middle of the second group of staves. Third movement, entitled *(Scherzo) Furiant* begins at the top of the following page and ends on page 81/82. The fourth movement, entitled *Finale*, begins on page 82/83 and ends in the middle of the second group of staves on page 110/111. After final double-line in the piano part the composer wrote the word *"Fine"*; on the right side a little lower, at the level of the piano left hand stave, there is the inscription *"Finished 3. 10. 1887 at Vysoká (at the village feast day) Antonín Dvořák."* The last page of music paper is empty.

b) Original edition published by N. Simrock, Berlin, Ed. No. 8859. Copyright is not mentioned.

The manuscript does not show any traces from which we could judge that it was used by the engraver; the publishing house may have obtained a copy of the manuscript for this purpose. The names of the instruments stand in the manuscript only before the **beginning** of the first movement (Violino I, Violino II, Viola, Cello, Piano-Forte). The manuscript does not obtain any metronomic indications. On the other hand, it contains a great number of insertions added by the composer in red ink and concerning mostly tempo, dynamics, pedalisation, phrasing etc. In some places even the music had been changed in this way. Exceptionally a few additional marks were inserted in black or blue pencil. Almost all these insertions are also contained in the original Simrock edition. This gives us reason to believe that the revision had been carried out by the composer before the copy of the manuscript for the use of the publishing house was procured.

Our edition is based on Simrock's print, published during the composer's lifetime and doubtlessly under his direct supervision. It has been carefully compared with the autograph. The more important deviations of the sources are listed in the Editorial Notes ("Annotazioni"). Obvious misprints have been corrected and details omitted in Simrock's edition have been added in accordance with the manuscript. Further, the missing interpretation marks have been added on the basis of analogous passages of the manuscript as well as of the print. The more important editors' addenda have been put within square brackets [ ].

ABBREVIATIONS:

A = the manuscript

S = Simrock's edition

Viol. I /Po, Viol. II/Po, Vla/Po, Vclo/Po = the part of the 1st or 2nd violin, viola or violoncello in the score

Po = the piano part in the score

m. d. = right hand

m. s. = left hand

Viol. I., Viol. II., Vla, Vclo = separate parts for the violin, viola or violoncello as published by Simrock

Versio I. = original version, the change having been carried out by the composer in the manuscript

T = bar

Large Arabic numerals indicate the bar; the small numbers beside them indicate the note (or chord) in the bar; rests are not counted.

ANNOTAZIONI

I

53 Po m. d. A : −, S : *espressivo*
59 Viol II/Po A : −, S : *dim.*

75 Viol I/Po, Po A : −, S : *leggiero*
103 Vclo/Po A, S : *arco*; SN ; − ; (vide 345)
111 Vclo/Po A, S : − ; SN : *arco*; (vide 353)

139$_{2, 6}$ Po m. s. A: *fis, a* − SN = S

190$_{5, 6}$ Po m. d. A: *ges² as²*; SN = S

240, 242 A: segue vide 1 T

273$_4$ Po m. d.
273$_3$ Po m. s. A: ∿

279 Po A: −, S: *tranquillo*

291 Po A: − ; S: *sostenuto;* SN = A

295 Po A: − S: *espresivo, largamente*

302 A: −, S: *Tempo I.*

303 A: *Tempo I.* S: −

316$_4$ Viol II/Po A, S: *d¹*; SN: *e¹* (vide 74)

345 Po A: −, S: *tranquillo*

423$_{2, 3}$ Po m. s. A: *e¹, gis¹*; SN = S

II

6 Vla/Po A: mp, S: *espressivo;* SN = S

11$_1$ Po m. d.
Po m. s. A: *tr.* S: *ten,*

64 Viol II/Po, Vla/Po A: −, S: *pizz.*

70 Viol II/Po, Vla/Po A: −, S: *arco*

150$_1$ Po m. d. A: cis³, S: *cis³*, SN: *c³* − (analog. 146$_1$)

165, 166$_{3, 4}$ Vla/Po A: *cis¹-e¹, cis¹-g¹;* SN = S (analog. 161, 162)

186 Po A: *p*, S:f

218$_{1-4}$ Po m. s. A: ♩♪♪♪♩ , S: ♪♪♪ , SN = A

221 Vla/Po, Vclo/Po A: −, S: *pizz.*

236$_4$ Vla/Po A: −, S: *arco*

294 Po A: −, S: *molto tranquillo*

III

73 A: Vers. I segue vide 2T analog. 72, S: − ; SN = S

IV

32$_{1-3}$ Viol II/Po A: *fis¹ c² h¹*, S: *c² h¹ fis¹*; SN = S

262−265 A: −, S: *poco sostenuto*, SN = S

266 A: −, S: *Tempo I*

288$_6$ Po m. d. A: *e²*, S: *c²*, SN = S (analog. 286$_6$)

365 A: segue vide 1 T., S: −

374−381 A: −, S: *poco sostenuto*, SN = S

382 Viol II/Po, Po A: − S: *tranquillo*, Viol II S: −

Dr Antonín Čubr

Antonín Dvořák

Chamber Works for
Piano and Strings

PIANO TRIO IN F MINOR, OP. 65

I

4. II. 1883

Piano Trio in F Minor

19. II. 1883

II

7. III. 1883

III

38   Piano Trio in F Minor

6. III. 1883

IV

FINALE

20. III. 1883

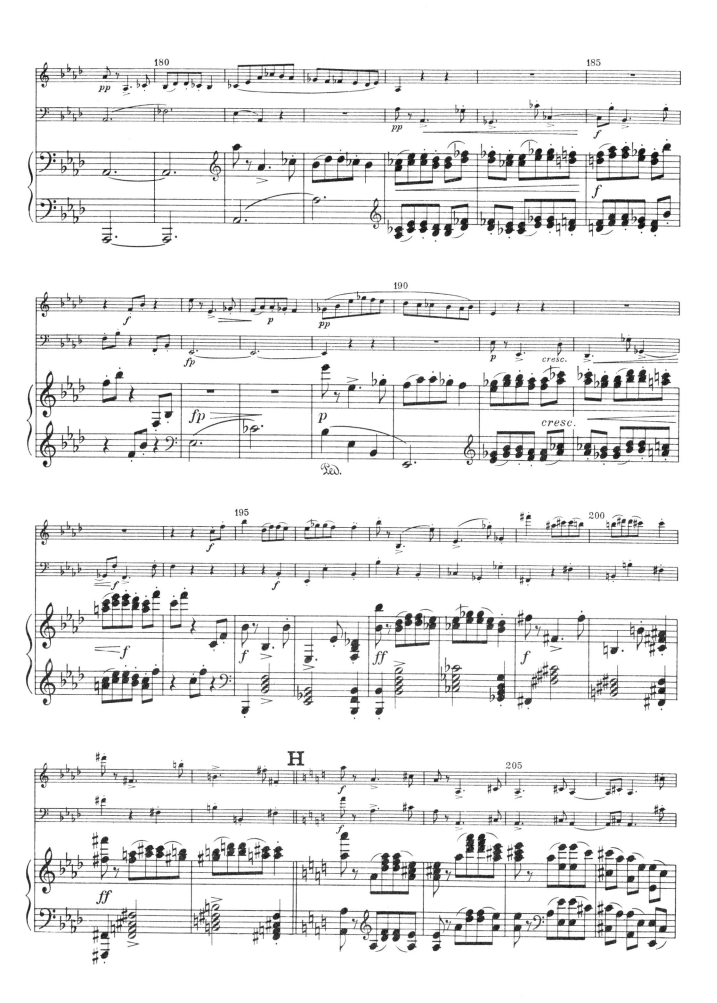

31. III. 1883

DUMKY TRIO, OP. 90

[I]

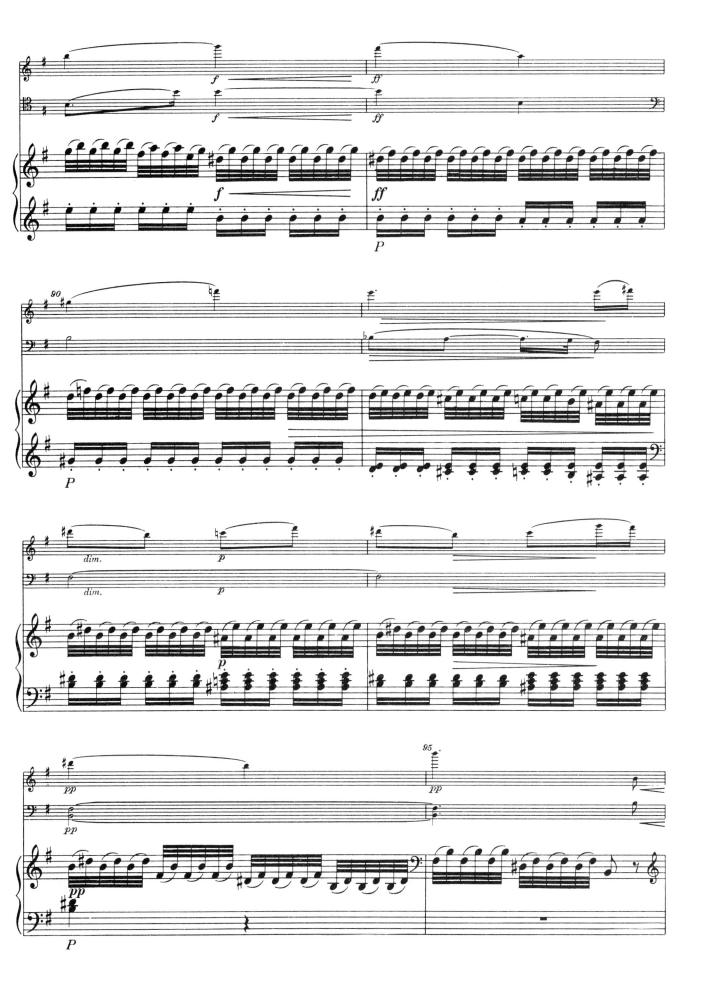

30. XI. 1890

[II]

[III]

[IV]

31. I. 1891

[VI]

12. II. 1891

PIANO QUARTET IN D MAJOR, OP. 23

I

24. V. 1875

126   Piano Quartet in D Major

30. V. 1875

II

VAR. IV.

VAR. V.

Quasi l'istesso tempo

III
FINALE

Allegro scherzando, quasi Tempo I.

Allegro scherzando, quasi Tempo I.

10. VI. 1875

PIANO QUARTET IN E-FLAT MAJOR, OP. 87

I

12. VII. 1889

II

III

D Un pochettino più mosso

Un pochettino più mosso

IV
FINALE

232   Piano Quartet in E-flat Major

242   Piano Quartet in E-flat Major

19. VIII. 1889

PIANO QUINTET IN A MAJOR, OP. 81

I

Piano Quintet in A Major

28. 8. 1887

II

DUMKA

Un pochettino più mosso

Vivace (quasi l'istesso tempo)

III

SCHERZO (FURIANT)

IV
FINALE